Kristen Suzanne's
EASY
Raw Vegan
Entrees

Delicious & Easy Raw Food Recipes for
Hearty & Satisfying Entrees
Like Lasagna, Burgers, Wraps,
Pasta, Ravioli, & Pizza

Plus Cheeses, Breads, Crackers,
Bars & Much More!

by Kristen Suzanne

*Green
Butterfly
Press*

Scottsdale, Arizona

OTHER BOOKS BY KRISTEN SUZANNE

- *Kristen's Raw: The EASY Way to Get Started & Succeed at the Raw Food Vegan Diet & Lifestyle*
- *Kristen Suzanne's EASY Raw Vegan Desserts*
- *Kristen Suzanne's EASY Raw Vegan Soups*
- *Kristen Suzanne's EASY Raw Vegan Salads & Dressings*
- *Kristen Suzanne's EASY Raw Vegan Sides & Snacks*
- *Kristen Suzanne's EASY Raw Vegan Smoothies, Juices, Elixirs & Drinks (includes wine drinks!)*
- *Kristen Suzanne's EASY Raw Vegan Holidays*
- *Kristen Suzanne's EASY Raw Vegan Dehydrating*
- *Kristen Suzanne's Ultimate Raw Vegan Hemp Recipes*

COMING SOON

- *Kristen Suzanne's Raw Vegan Diet for EASY Weight Loss*
- *Kristen Suzanne's Ultimate Raw Vegan Chocolate Recipes*

For details, Raw Food resources, and Kristen's free Raw Food newsletter, please visit:

KristensRaw.com

For information on excerpting, reprinting or licensing portions of this book, please write to info@greenbutterflypress.com.

Green Butterfly Press
19550 N. Gray Hawk Drive, Suite 1042
Scottsdale, AZ 85255 USA

Library of Congress Control Number: 2008941404
Library of Congress Subject Heading:
1. Cookery (Natural foods) 2. Raw foods

ISBN: 978-0-9817556-3-2

1.2

CONTENTS

CHAPTER 1

RAW BASICS

NOTE: "Raw Basics" is a brief introduction to Raw for those who are new to the subject. It is the same in all of my recipe books. If you have recently read this section in one of them, you may wish to skip to Chapter 2.

WHY RAW?

Living the Raw vegan lifestyle has made me a more effective person... in everything I do. I get to experience pure, sustainable all-day-long energy. My body is in perfect shape and I gain strength and endurance in my exercise routine with each passing day. My relationships are the best they've ever been, because I'm happy and I love myself and my life. My headaches have ceased to exist, and my skin glows with the radiance of brand new life, which is exactly how I feel. Raw vegan is the best thing that has ever happened to me.

Whatever your passion is in life (family, business, exercise, meditation, hobbies, etc.), eating Raw vegan will take it to unbelievable new heights. Raw vegan food offers you the most amazing benefits – physically, mentally, and spiritually. It is *the* ideal choice for your food consumption if you want to become the healthiest and best "you" possible. Raw vegan food is for people who want to live longer while feeling younger. It's for people who want to feel vibrant and alive, and want to enjoy life like never before. All I ever have to say to someone is, "Just try it for yourself." It will change your life. From simple to gourmet, there's always something for everyone, and it's delicious. Come into the world of Raw with me, and experience for yourself the most amazing health *ever*.

Are you ready for your new lease on life? The time is now. Let's get started!

SOME GREAT THINGS TO KNOW BEFORE DIVING INTO THESE RECIPES

Organic Food

I use organic produce and products for pretty much everything. There are very few exceptions, and that would be if the recipe called for something I just can't get organic such as jicama, young Thai coconuts, certain seasonings, or any random ingredient that my local health food store is not able to procure from an organic grower for whatever reason.

If you think organic foods are too expensive, then start in baby steps and buy a few things at a time. Realize that you're going to be spending less money in the long run on health problems as your health improves, and going organic is one way to facilitate that. I find that once people learn about the direct cause-and-effect relationship between non-organic food and illnesses such as cancer, the relatively small premium you pay for organic becomes a trivial non-issue. Your health is worth it!

Choosing organically grown foods is one of the most important choices we can make. The more people who choose organic, the lower the prices will be in the long run. Vote with your dollar! Here is something I do to help further this cause and you can, too... whenever I eat at a restaurant I always write on the bill, "I would eat here more if you served organic food." Can you imagine what would happen if we all did this?

It's essential to use organic ingredients for many reasons:

1. The health benefits – superior nutrition, reduced intake of chemicals and heavy metals and decreased exposure to carcinogens. Organic food has been shown to have up to 300% more nutrition than conventionally grown, non-organic produce.

2. To have the very best tasting food ever! I've had people tell me in my classes that they never knew vegetables tasted so good – and it's because I only use organic.

3. Greater variety of heirloom fruits and vegetables.

4. Cleaner rivers and waterways for our earth, along with minimized topsoil erosion.

Going Organic on a Budget

Going organic on a budget is not impossible. Here are things to keep in mind that will help you afford it:

1. Buy in bulk. Ask the store you frequent if they'll give you a deal for buying certain foods by the case. (Just make sure it's a case of something that you can go through in a timely fashion so it doesn't go to waste). Consider this for bananas or greens especially if you drink lots of smoothies or green juice, like I do.

2. See if local neighbors, family or friends will share the price of getting cases of certain foods. When you do this, you can go beyond your local grocery store and contact great places (which deliver nationally) such as Boxed Greens (BoxedGreens.com) or Diamond Organics (DiamondOrganics.com). Maybe they'll extend a discount if your order goes above a certain

amount or if you get certain foods by the case. It never hurts to ask.

3. Pay attention to organic foods that are not very expensive to buy relative to the conventional prices (bananas, for example). Load up on those.

4. Be smart when picking what you buy as organic. Some conventionally grown foods have higher levels of pesticides than others. For those, go organic. Then, for foods that are not sprayed as much, you can go conventional. Avocados, for example, aren't sprayed too heavily so you could buy those as conventional. Here is a resource that keeps an updated list:

foodnews.org/walletguide.php

5. Buy produce that is on sale. Pay attention to which organic foods are on sale for the week and plan your menu around that. Every little bit adds up!

6. Grow your own sprouts. Load up on these for salads, soups, and smoothies. Very inexpensive. Buy the organic seeds in the bulk bins at your health food store or buy online and grow them yourself. Fun!

7. Buy organic seeds/nuts in bulk online and freeze. Nuts and seeds typically get less expensive when you order in bulk from somewhere like Sun Organic (SunOrganic.com). Take advantage of this and freeze them (they'll last the year!). Do the same with dried fruits/dates/etc. And remember, when you make a recipe that calls for expensive nuts, you can often easily replace them with a less expensive seed such as sunflower or pumpkin seeds.

8. Buy seasonally; hence, don't buy a bunch of organic berries out of season (i.e., eat more apples and bananas in the fall and winter). Also, consider buying frozen organic fruits, especially when they're on sale!

9. Be content with minimal variety. Organic spinach banana smoothies are inexpensive. So, having this most mornings for your breakfast can save you money. You can change it up for fun by adding cinnamon one day, nutmeg another, vanilla extract yet another. Another inexpensive meal or snack is a spinach apple smoothie. Throw in a date or some raisins for extra pizazz. It helps the budget when you make salads, smoothies, and soups with ingredients that tend to be less expensive such as carrots (year round), bananas (year round), zucchini and cucumbers (in the summer), etc.

Kristen Suzanne's Tip: A Note About Herbs

Hands down, fresh herbs taste the best and have the highest nutritional value. While I recommend fresh herbs whenever possible, you can substitute dried herbs if necessary. But do so in a ratio of:

3 parts fresh to 1 part dried

Dried herbs impart a more concentrated flavor, which is why you need less of them. For instance, if your recipe calls for three tablespoons of fresh basil, you'll be fine if you use one tablespoon of dried basil instead.

The Infamous Salt Question: What Kind Do I Use?

All life on earth began in the oceans, so it's no surprise that organisms' cellular fluids chemically resemble sea water. Saltwater in the ocean is "salty" due to many, many minerals, not just sodium chloride. We need these minerals, not coincidentally, in roughly the same proportion that they exist in... guess where?... the ocean! (You've just gotta love Mother Nature.)

So when preparing food, I always use sea salt, which can be found at any health food store. Better still is sea salt that was deposited into salt beds before the industrial revolution started spewing toxins into the world's waterways. My personal preference is Himalayan Crystal Salt, fine granules. It's mined high in the mountains from ancient sea-beds, has a beautiful pink color, and imparts more than 84 essential minerals into your diet. You can use either the Himalayan crystal variety or Celtic Sea Salt, but I would highly recommend sticking to at least one of these two. You can buy Himalayan crystal salt through KristensRaw.com/store.

Kristen Suzanne's Tip: Start Small with Strong Flavors

FLAVORS AND THEIR STRENGTH

There are certain flavors and ingredients that are particularly strong, such as garlic, ginger, onion, and salt. It's important to observe patience here, as these are flavors that can be loved or considered offensive, depending on who is eating the food. I know people who want the maximum amount of salt called for in a recipe and I know some who are highly sensitive to it. Therefore, to make the best possible Raw experience for you, I recommend starting on the "small end" especially with ingredients like garlic, ginger, strong savory herbs and seasonings, onions (any variety), citrus, and even salt. If I've given you a range in a recipe, for instance *1/4 - 1/2 teaspoon Himalayan crystal salt* then I recommend starting with the smaller amount, and then tasting it. If you don't love it, then add a little more of that ingredient and taste it again. Start small. It's worth the extra 60 seconds it might take you to do this. You might end up using less, saving it for the next recipe you make and voila, you're saving a little money.

Lesson #1: It's very hard to correct any flavors of excess, so start small and build.

Lesson #2: Write it down. When an ingredient offers a "range" for itself, write down the amount you liked best. If you use an "optional" ingredient, make a note about that as well.

One more thing to know about some strong flavors like the ones mentioned above... with Raw food, these flavors can intensify the finished product as each day passes. For example, the garlic in your soup, on the day you made it, might be perfect. On day two, it's still really great but a little stronger in flavor. And by day three, you might want to carry around your toothbrush or a little chewing gum!

HERE IS A TIP TO HELP CONTROL THIS

If you're making a recipe in advance, such as a dressing or soup that you won't be eating until the following day or even the day after that, then hold off on adding some of the strong seasonings until the day you eat it (think garlic and ginger). Or, if you're going to make the dressing or soup in advance, use less of the strong seasoning, knowing that it might intensify on its own by the time you eat it. This isn't a huge deal because it doesn't change that dramatically, but I mention it so you won't be surprised, especially when serving a favorite dish to others.

Kristen Suzanne's Tip: Doubling Recipes

More often than not, there are certain ingredients and flavors that you don't typically double in their entirety, if you're making a double or triple batch of a recipe. These are strong-flavored ingredients similar to those mentioned above (salt, garlic, ginger, herbs, seasoning, etc). A good rule of thumb is this: For a double batch, use 1.5 times the amount for certain ingredients. Taste it and see if you need the rest. For instance, if I'm making a "double batch" of soup, and the normal recipe calls for 1 tablespoon of Himalayan crystal salt, then I'll put in 1 1/2 tablespoons to start, instead of two. Then, I'll taste it and add the remaining 1/2 tablespoon, if necessary.

This same principle is not necessarily followed when dividing a recipe in half. Go ahead and simply divide in half, or by whatever amount you're making. If there is a range for a particular ingredient provided, I still recommend that you use the smaller amount of an ingredient when dividing. Taste the final product and then decide whether or not to add more.

My recipes provide a variety of yields, as you'll see below. Some recipes make 2 servings and some make 4 - 6 servings. For those of you making food for only yourself, then simply cut the recipes making 4 - 6 servings in half. Or, as I always do... I make the larger serving size and then I have enough food for a couple of meals. If a recipe yields 2 servings, I usually double it for the same reason.

Kristen Suzanne's Tip: Changing Produce

"But I made it exactly like this last time! Why doesn't it taste the same?"

Here is something you need to embrace when preparing Raw vegan food. Fresh produce can vary in its composition of water, and even flavor, to some degree. There are times I've made marinara sauce and, to me, it was the perfect level of sweetness in the finished product. Then, the next time I made it, you would have thought I added a smidge of sweetener. This is due to the fact that fresh Raw produce can have a slightly different taste from time to time when you make a recipe (only ever so slightly, so don't be alarmed). *Aahhh, here is the silver lining!* This means you'll never get bored living the Raw vegan lifestyle because your recipes can change a little in flavor from time to time, even though you followed the same recipe. Embrace this natural aspect of produce and love it for everything that it is. ☺

This is much less of an issue with cooked food. Most of the water is taken out of cooked food, so you typically get the same flavors and experience each and every time. Boring!

Kristen Suzanne's Tip: Ripeness and Storage for Your Fresh Produce

1. I never use green bell peppers because they are not "ripe." This is why so many people have a hard time digesting them (often "belching" after eating them). To truly experience the greatest health, it's important to eat fruits and vegetables at their peak ripeness. Therefore, make sure you only use red, orange, or yellow bell peppers. Store these in your refrigerator.

2. A truly ripe banana has some brown freckles or spots on the peel. This is when you're supposed to eat a banana. Store these on your countertop away from other produce, because bananas give off a gas as they ripen, which will affect the ripening process of your other produce. And, if you have a lot of bananas, split them up. This will help prevent all of your bananas from ripening at once.

3. Keep avocados on the counter until they reach ripeness (when their skin is usually brown in color and if you gently squeeze it, it "gives" just a little). At this point, you can put them in the refrigerator where they'll last up to a week longer. If you keep ripe avocados on the counter, they'll only last another couple of days. Avocados, like bananas, give off a gas as they ripen, which will affect the ripening process of your other produce. Let them ripen away from your other produce. And, if you have a lot of avocados, separate them. This will help prevent all of your avocados from ripening at once.

4. Tomatoes are best stored on your counter. Do not put them in the refrigerator or they'll get a "mealy" texture.

5. Pineapple is ripe for eating when you can gently pull a leaf out of the top of it. Therefore, test your pineapple for ripeness at the store to ensure you're buying the sweetest one possible. Just pull one of the leaves out from the top. After 3 to 4 attempts on different leaves, if you can't gently take one of them out, then move on to another pineapple.

6. Stone fruits (fruits with pits, such as peaches, plums, and nectarines), bananas and avocados all continue to ripen after being picked.

7. I have produce ripening all over my house. Sounds silly maybe, but I don't want it crowded on my kitchen countertop. I move it around and turn it over daily.

For a more complete list of produce ripening tips, check out my book, *Kristen's Raw,* available at Amazon.com.

Kristen Suzanne's Tip: Proper Dehydration Techniques

Dehydrating your Raw vegan food at a low temperature is a technique that warms and dries the food while preserving its nutritional integrity. When using a dehydrator, it is recommended that you begin the dehydrating process at a temperature of 130 - 140 degrees for about an hour. Then, lower the temperature to 105 degrees for the remaining time of dehydration. Using a high temperature such as 140 degrees, *in the initial stages of dehydration*, does not destroy the nutritional value of the food. During this initial phase, the food does the most "sweating" (releasing moisture), which cools the food. Therefore, while the temperature of the air circulating *around* the food is about 140 degrees, the food itself is much cooler. These directions apply only when using an Excalibur Dehydrator because of their Horizontal-Airflow Drying System. Furthermore, I am happy to only recommend Excalibur dehydrators because of their first-class products and customer service. For details, visit the *Raw Kitchen Essential Tools* section of my website at KristensRaw.com/store.

MY YIELD AND SERVING AMOUNTS NOTED IN THE RECIPES

Each recipe in this book shows an approximate amount that the recipe yields (the quantity it makes). I find that "one serving" to me might be considered two servings to someone else, or vice versa. Therefore, I tried to use an "average" when listing the serving amount. Don't let that stop you from eating a two-serving dish in one sitting, if it seems like the right amount for you. It simply depends on how hungry you are.

WHAT IS THE DIFFERENCE BETWEEN CHOPPED, DICED, AND MINCED?

Chop

This gives relatively uniform cuts, but doesn't need to be perfectly neat or even. You'll often be asked to chop something before putting it into a blender or food processor, which is why it doesn't have to be uniform size since it'll be getting blended or pureed.

Dice

This produces a nice cube shape, and can be different sizes, depending on which you prefer. This is great for vegetables.

Mince

This produces an even, very fine cut, typically used for fresh herbs, onions, garlic and ginger.

Julienne

This is a fancy term for long, rectangular cuts.

WHAT EQUIPMENT DO I NEED FOR MY NEW RAW FOOD KITCHEN?

I go into much more detail regarding the perfect setup for your Raw vegan kitchen in my book, *Kristen's Raw,* which is a must read for anybody who wants to learn the easy ways to succeed with living the Raw vegan lifestyle. Here are the main pieces of equipment you'll want to get you going:

1. An excellent chef's knife (6 - 8 inches in length – non-serrated). Of everything you do with Raw food, you'll be chopping and cutting the most, so invest in a great knife. This truly makes doing all the chopping really fun!

2. Blender

3. Food Processor (get a 7 or 10-cup or more)

4. Juicer

5. Spiralizer or Turning Slicer

6. Dehydrator – Excalibur® is the best company by far and is available at KristensRaw.com

7. Salad spinner

8. Other knives (paring, serrated)

For links to online retailers that sell my favorite kitchen tools and foods, visit KristensRaw.com/store.

SOAKING AND DEHYDRATING NUTS AND SEEDS

This is an important topic. When using nuts and seeds in Raw vegan foods, you'll find that recipes sometimes call for them to be "soaked" or "soaked and dehydrated." Here is the low-down on the importance and the difference between the two.

Why Should You Soak Your Nuts and Seeds?

Most nuts and seeds come packed by Mother Nature with enzyme inhibitors, rendering them harder to digest. These inhibitors essentially shut down the nuts' and seeds' metabolic activity, rendering them dormant – for as long as they need to be – until they detect a moisture-rich environment that's suitable for germination (e.g., rain). By soaking your nuts and seeds, you trick the nuts into "waking up," shutting off the inhibitors so that the enzymes can become active. This greatly enhances the nuts' digestibility for you and is highly recommended if you want to experience Raw vegan food in the healthiest way possible.

14

Even though you'll want to soak the nuts to activate their enzymes, before using them, you'll need to re-dry them and grind them down anywhere from coarse to fine (into a powder almost like flour), depending on the recipe. To dry them, you'll need a dehydrator. (If you don't own a dehydrator yet, then, if a recipe calls for "soaked and dehydrated," just skip the soaking part; you can use the nuts or seeds in the dry form that you bought them).

Drying your nuts (but not yet grinding them) is a great thing to do before storing them in the freezer or refrigerator (preferably in glass mason jars). They will last a long time and you'll always have them on hand, ready to use.

In my recipes, always use nuts and seeds that are "soaked and dehydrated" (that is, *dry*) unless otherwise stated as "soaked" (wet).

Some nuts and seeds don't have to follow the enzyme inhibitor rule; therefore, they don't need to be soaked. These are:

- Macadamia nuts
- Brazil nuts
- Pine nuts
- Hemp seeds
- Most cashews

An additional note... there are times when the recipe will call for soaking, even though it's for a type of nut or seed without enzyme inhibitors, such as Brazil nuts. The logic behind this is to help *soften* the nuts so they blend into a smoother texture, especially if you don't have a high-powered blender. This is helpful when making nut milks, soups and sauces.

Instructions for "Soaking" and "Soaking and Dehydrating" Nuts

"Soaking"

The general rule to follow: Any nuts or seeds that require soaking can be soaked overnight (6 - 10 hours). Put the required amount of nuts or seeds into a bowl and add enough water to cover by about an inch or so. Set them on your counter overnight. The following morning, or 6 - 10 hours after you soaked them, drain and rinse them. They are now ready to eat or use in a recipe. At this point, they need to be refrigerated in an airtight container (preferably a glass mason jar) and they'll have a shelf life of about 3 days maximum. Only soak the amount you're going to need or eat, unless you plan on dehydrating them right away.

A note about flax seeds and chia seeds... these don't need to be soaked if your recipe calls for grinding them into a powder. Some recipes will call to soak the seeds in their "whole-seed" form, before making crackers and bread, because they create a very gelatinous and binding texture when soaked. You can soak flax or chia seeds in a ratio of one-part seeds to two-parts water, and they can be soaked for as short as 1 hour and up to 12 hours. At this point, they are ready to use (don't drain them). Personally, when I use flax seeds, I usually grind them and don't soak them. It's hard for your body to digest "whole" flax seeds, even if they are soaked. It's much easier for your body to assimilate the nutrients when they're ground to a flax meal.

"Soaking and Dehydrating"

Follow the same directions for soaking. Then, after draining and rinsing the nuts, spread them out on a mesh

16

dehydrator sheet and dehydrate them at 140 degrees for one hour. Lower the temperature to 105 degrees and dehydrate them until they're completely dry, which can take up to 24 hours.

Please note, all nuts and seeds called for in my recipes will always be "Raw and Organic" and "Soaked and Dehydrated" unless the recipe calls for soaking.

ALMOND PULP

Some of my recipes call for "almond pulp," which is really easy to make. After making your fresh almond milk (see *Nut/Seed Milk* recipe, p. 25) and straining it through a "nut milk bag," (available at NaturalZing.com or you can use a paint strainer bag from the hardware store – much cheaper), you will find a nice, soft pulp inside the bag. Turn the bag inside out and flatten the pulp out onto a paraflex dehydrator sheet with a spatula or your hand. Dehydrate the pulp at 140 degrees for one hour, then lower the temperature to 105 degrees and continue dehydrating until the almond pulp is dry (up to 24 hours). Break the pulp into chunks and store in the freezer until you're ready to use it. Before using the almond pulp, grind it into a flour in your blender or food processor.

SOY LECITHIN

Some recipes (desserts, in particular) will call for soy lecithin, which is extracted from soybean oil. This optional ingredient is not Raw. If you use soy lecithin, I highly recommend using a brand that is "non-GMO," meaning it was processed without any genetically modified ingredients (a great brand is Health Alliance®). Soy lecithin helps your dessert (cheesecake, for example) maintain a firmer texture.

That said, it's certainly not necessary. If an amount isn't suggested, a good rule of thumb is to use 1 teaspoon per 1 cup total recipe volume.

ICE CREAM FLAVORINGS

When making Raw vegan ice cream, it's better to use alcohol-free extracts so they freeze better.

SWEETENERS

The following is a list of sweeteners that you might see used in my recipes. It's important to know that the healthiest sweeteners are fresh whole fruits, including fresh dates. That said, dates sometimes compromise texture in recipes. As a chef, I look for great texture, and as a health food advocate, I lean towards fresh dates. But as a consultant helping people embrace a Raw vegan lifestyle, I'm also supportive of helping them transition, which sometimes means using raw agave nectar, or some other easy-to-use sweetener that might not have the healthiest ranking in the Raw food world, but is still much healthier than most sweeteners used in the Standard American Diet.

Most of my recipes can use pitted dates in place of raw agave nectar. There is some debate among Raw food enthusiasts as to whether agave nectar is Raw. The company I use (Madhava®) claims to be Raw and says they do not heat their Raw agave nectar above 118 degrees. If however, you still want to eat the healthiest of sweeteners, then bypass the raw agave nectar and use pitted dates. In most recipes, you can simply substitute 1 - 2 pitted dates for 1 tablespoon of raw agave nectar. Dates won't give you a super creamy texture, but the texture can be improved by making a "date paste" (pureeing pitted and soaked dates – with their soak water, plus some additional water, if necessary – in a food processor fitted with the "S" blade). This, of course, takes a little extra time.

If using raw agave nectar is easier and faster for you, then go ahead and use it; just be sure to buy the Raw version that says they don't heat the agave above 118 degrees (see KristensRaw.com/store for links to this product). And, again, if you're looking to go as far as you can on the spectrum of health, then I recommend using pitted dates. Most of my recipes say raw agave nectar because that is most convenient for people.

Agave Nectar

There are a variety of agave nectars on the market, but again, not all of them are Raw. Make sure it is labeled "Raw" on the bottle *as well as claiming that it isn't processed above 118 degrees.* Just because the label says "Raw" does not necessarily mean it is so... do a double check and make sure it also claims not to be heated above the 118 degrees cut-off. Agave nectar is noteworthy for having a low glycemic index.

Dates

Dates are probably the healthiest of sweeteners, because they're a fresh whole food. Fresh organic dates are filled with nutrition, including calcium and magnesium. I like to call dates, "Nature's Candy."

Feel free to use dates instead of agave or honey in Raw vegan recipes. If a recipe calls for 1/2 cup of raw agave, then you can substitute with approximately 1/2 cup of pitted dates. You can also make your own date sugar by dehydrating pitted dates and then grinding them down. This is a great alternative to Rapadura®.

Honey

Most honey is technically raw, but it is not vegan by most definitions of "vegan" because it is produced by animals, who therefore are at risk of being mistreated. While honey does not have the health risks associated with animal byproducts such as eggs or dairy, it can spike the body's natural sugar levels. Agave nectar has a lower, healthier glycemic index and can replace any recipe you find that calls for honey, in a 1 to 1 ratio.

Maple Syrup

Maple syrup is made from boiled sap of the maple tree. It is not considered Raw, but some people still use it as a sweetener in certain dishes.

Rapadura®

This is a dried sugarcane juice, and it's not Raw. It is, however, an unrefined and unbleached organic whole-cane sugar. It imparts a nice deep sweetness to your recipes, even if you only use a little. Feel free to omit it if you'd like to adhere to a strictly Raw program. You can substitute Rapadura with home-made date sugar (see Dates above).

Stevia

This is from the leaf of the stevia plant. It has a sweet taste and doesn't elevate blood sugar levels. It's very sweet, so you'll want to use much less stevia than you would any other sweetener. My mom actually grows her own stevia. It's a great addition in fresh smoothies, for example, to add some sweetness without the calories. You can use the white powdered or liquid version from the store, but these are not Raw. When possible, the best way to have stevia is grow it yourself.

Yacon Syrup

This sweetener has a low glycemic index, making it very attractive to some people. It has a molasses-type flavor that is nice and rich. You can replace raw agave with this sweetener in my recipes, but make sure to get the Raw variety, available at NaturalZing.com. They offer a few different yacon syrups, including one in particular that is not heat-treated. Be sure to choose that one.

SUN-DRIED TOMATOES

By far, the best sun-dried tomatoes are those you make yourself with a dehydrator. If you don't have a dehydrator, make sure you buy the "dry" sun-dried tomatoes, usually found in the bulk section of your health food market. Don't buy the kind that are packed in a jar of oil.

Also... don't buy sun-dried tomatoes if they're really dark (almost black) because these just don't taste as good. Again, I recommend making them yourself if you truly want the freshest flavor possible. It's really fun to do!

EATING WITH YOUR EYES

Most of us, if not all, naturally eat with our eyes before taking a bite of food. So, do yourself a favor and make your eating experience the best ever with the help of a simple, gorgeous presentation. Think of it this way, with real estate, it's always *location, location, location*, right? Well, with food, it's always *presentation, presentation, presentation.*

Luckily, Raw food does this on its own with all of its naturally vibrant and bright colors. But I take it even one step farther – I use my best dishes when I eat. I use my beautiful wine glasses for my smoothies and juices. I use my fancy goblets for many of my desserts. Why? Because I'm worth it. And, so are you! Don't save your good china just for company. Believe me, you'll notice the difference. Eating well is an attitude, and when you take care of yourself, your body will respond in kind.

ONLINE RESOURCES FOR GREAT PRODUCTS

For a complete and detailed list of my favorite kitchen tools, products, and various foods (all available online), please visit: KristensRaw.com/store.

BOOK RECOMMENDATIONS

I highly recommend reading the following life-changing books.

- *Diet for a New America*, by John Robbins
- *The Food Revolution*, by John Robbins
- *The China Study*, by T. Colin Campbell
- *Skinny Bitch*, by Rory Freedman

MEASUREMENT CONVERSIONS

1 tablespoon = 3 teaspoons

1 ounce = 2 tablespoons

1/4 cup = 4 tablespoons

1/3 cup = 5 1/3 tablespoons

1 cup

= 8 ounces

= 16 tablespoons

= 1/2 pint

1/2 quart

= 1 pint

= 2 cups

1 gallon

= 4 quarts

= 8 pints

= 16 cups

= 128 ounces

BASIC RECIPES TO KNOW

Nourishing Rejuvelac

Yield 1 gallon

Rejuvelac is a cheesy-tasting liquid that is rich in enzymes and healthy flora to support a healthy intestine and digestion.

Get comfortable making this super easy recipe because its use goes beyond just drinking it between meals.

1 cup soft wheat berries, rye berries, or a mixture

water

Place the wheat berries in a half-gallon jar and fill the jar with water. Screw the lid on the jar and soak the wheat berries overnight(10 - 12 hours) on your counter. The next morning, drain and rinse them. Sprout the wheat berries for 2 days, draining and rinsing 1 - 2 times a day.

Then, fill the jar with purified water and screw on the lid, or cover with cheesecloth secured with a rubber band. Allow to ferment for 24 - 36 hours, or until the desired tartness is achieved. It should have a cheesy, almost tart/lemony flavor and scent.

Strain your rejuvelac into another glass jar and store in the refrigerator for up to 5 - 7 days. For a second batch using the same sprouted wheat berries, fill the same jar of already sprouted berries with water again, and allow to ferment for 24 hours. Strain off the rejuvelac as you did the time before this. You can do this process yet again, noting that each time the rejuvelac gets a little weaker in flavor.

Enjoy 1/4 - 1 cup of *Nourishing Rejuvelac* first thing in the morning and/or between meals. It's best to start with a small amount and work your way up as your body adjusts.

Suggestion:

- For extra nutrition and incredible flavor, *Nourishing Rejuvelac* can be used in various recipes such as Raw vegan cheeses, desserts, smoothies, soups, dressings and more. Simply use it in place of the water required by the recipe.

Crème Fraiche

Yield approximately 2 cups

> 1 cup cashews, soaked 1 hour, drained, and rinsed
> 1/4 - 1/2 cup *Nourishing Rejuvelac* (see p. 23)
> 1 - 2 tablespoons raw agave nectar

Blend the ingredients until smooth. Store in an airtight glass mason jar for up to 5 days. This freezes well, so feel free to make a double batch for future use.

Nut/Seed Milk (regular)

Yield 4 - 5 cups

The creamiest nut/seed milk traditionally comes from hemp seeds, cashews, pine nuts, Brazil nuts or macadamia nuts, although I'm also a huge fan of milks made from walnuts, pecans, hazelnuts, almonds, sesame seeds, and others.

This recipe does not include a sweetener, but when I'm in the mood for a little sweetness, I add a couple of pitted dates or a squirt of raw agave nectar. Yum!

> 1 1/2 cups nuts, soaked 6 - 12 hours, drained and rinsed
> 3 1/4 cups water
> pinch Himalayan crystal salt, optional

Blend the ingredients until smooth and deliciously creamy. For an even *extra creamy* texture, strain your nut/seed milk through a nut milk bag.

Sweet Nut/Seed Cream (thick)

Yield 2 - 3 cups

> 1 cup nuts or seeds, soaked 6 - 8 hours, drained and rinsed
>
> 1 - 1 1/2 cups water, more if needed
>
> 2 - 3 tablespoons raw agave nectar or 2 - 3 dates, pitted
>
> 1/2 teaspoon vanilla extract, optional

Blend all of the ingredients until smooth.

Raw Mustard

Yield approximately 1 1/2 - 2 cups

> 1 - 2 tablespoons yellow mustard seeds (depending on how "hot" you want it), soaked 1 - 2 hours
>
> 1 1/2 cups extra virgin olive oil or hemp oil
>
> 1 1/2 tablespoons dry mustard powder
>
> 2 tablespoons apple cider vinegar
>
> 2 tablespoons fresh lemon juice
>
> 3 dates, pitted and soaked 30-minutes, drained
>
> 1/2 cup raw agave nectar
>
> 1 teaspoon Himalayan crystal salt
>
> pinch turmeric

Blend all of the ingredients together until smooth. It might be very thick, so if you want, add some water or oil to help thin it out. Adding more oil will help reduce the "heat" if it's too spicy for your taste.

Variation:

- *Honey Mustard Version:* Add another 1/3 cup raw agave nectar (or more, depending on how sweet you want it)

My Basic Raw Mayonnaise

Yield about 2 1/2 cups

People tell me all the time how much they like this recipe.

1 cup cashews, soaked 1 - 2 hours, drained
1/2 teaspoon paprika
2 cloves garlic
1 teaspoon onion powder
3 tablespoons fresh lemon juice
1/4 cup extra virgin olive oil or hemp oil
2 tablespoons parsley, chopped
2 tablespoons water, if needed

Blend all of the ingredients, except the parsley, until creamy. Pulse in the parsley. *My Basic Raw Mayonnaise* will stay fresh for up to one week in the refrigerator.

CHAPTER 2

IT'S RECIPE TIME!

Many of these recipes can be altered in small ways to create surprisingly different dishes. So, wherever available, be sure to look at the recipe's suggestions and variations prior to planning your menu or doing your food shopping.

SUN-DRIED TOMATO PUREE

Yield approximately 1 cup

Fasten your seat belts. When you taste this you'll think you've landed in Rome. Ma-Ma-Mia.

1 cup sun-dried tomatoes, soaked in red wine or water, 1 hour, drained

1 tablespoon apple cider vinegar

1/2 cup extra virgin olive oil

2 cloves garlic, pressed

3 tablespoons fresh thyme leaves or 1 tablespoon dried

1/4 - 1/2 teaspoon Himalayan crystal salt, or more to taste

1/4 teaspoon black pepper

Puree all of the ingredients in a food processor, fitted with the "S" blade. With the machine running, add a little water as necessary to make the puree the consistency of thick ketchup.

Serving suggestions:

- Serve on top of spiralized celery root or zucchini noodles for Raw pasta
- Fill zucchini boats for a delicious meal
- Use as a dip for vegetable crudités (or flax crackers) and take to a party
- Roll in a collard green, with some fresh chopped veggies sprinkled with minced olives, for an awesome sandwich to fill even the hungriest of tummies

ESSENCE OF SWEET ROSE DISH (fat-free)

Yield 2 servings

My mom loves the flavor of rose water, so she's always asking me to make this dish for her when I visit. (Beauty Tip: I love using rose water on an organic cotton ball as a toner for my face.)

The Sauce

8 - 10 dates, pitted, soaked 30 minutes, drained

2 tablespoons fresh lemon juice

1 - 2 tablespoons rose water, or more depending on preference*

1/2 teaspoon ground ginger

1/4 teaspoon allspice

water, as needed

The Vegetables

2 zucchini, spiralized or thinly sliced

1/4 cup red onion, minced

1 head of fennel, sliced

In a food processor, fitted with the "S" blade, puree the dates with the lemon juice and rose water, adding enough water to make a creamy paste. Add the ginger and allspice and pulse to combine. Serve over the vegetables.

* Available at most Middle Eastern markets, online, and in some Whole Foods Markets.

OLIVE CAPER EXTRAVAGANZA

Yield approximately 2 cups

I could make an entire meal from eating this with a plate full of fresh vegetables.

1/4 cup extra virgin olive oil

3/4 cup sun-dried tomatoes, soaked in red wine or water 1 hour, drained and chopped

1/2 cup kalamata olives, pitted

1/2 cup fresh basil, chopped

1/4 cup capers, rinsed and drained

1/4 cup fresh parsley, chopped

2 tablespoons fresh oregano, chopped

pinch cinnamon

Himalayan crystal salt, to taste

black pepper, to taste

Pulse all of the ingredients together in a food processor, fitted with the "S" blade, adding more oil (or water) as needed.

Serving suggestions:

- This is fantastic on a Raw pizza with Raw cheese
- Serve on top of angel hair zucchini pasta and toss to mix for a fabulous entrée
- Stuff into zucchini or cucumber boats and serve with 2 pieces of *Kristen Suzanne's Addictive Savory Mustard Bread* (see recipe, p. 83) for a delicious meal
- Fill half of a seeded tomato or two (or three!)

CAJUN PORTABELLAS WITH WILD RICE

Yield 2 servings

This spicy dish is fabulous with or without the rice. If you'd rather not have the rice, then enjoy the portabellas by themselves or on top of spiralized zucchini.

3/4 cup wild rice*

3 - 4 cups water

4 medium - large portabella mushrooms, cleaned and sliced

3/4 cup extra virgin olive oil

2 cloves garlic, pressed

1 1/2 teaspoons Himalayan crystal salt

2 teaspoons paprika

1 tablespoon garlic powder

2 teaspoons onion powder

(continued)

32

1/2 teaspoon black pepper

1/4 - 1/2 teaspoon cayenne pepper (depending on how spicy you want it)

1 tablespoon dried basil

1 tablespoon dried thyme

1 cup Roma tomatoes, diced (with juice and seeds)

Put the rice in a half-gallon jar with water and cover with a lid. Place the sealed jar in a dehydrator, and warm at 105 degrees for 24 hours. Drain the rice well and give a light rinse.

Place the portabellas with the olive oil, garlic and salt and set aside to marinate for 15 - 20 minutes. Take them out of the bowl (draining them) and place them in a new, clean bowl and add the remaining ingredients, except the tomatoes and rice. Toss well. Place on a paraflex dehydrator sheet and dehydrate at 140 degrees for up to 2 hours. Combine with the tomatoes and rice.

* Available at WildernessFamilyNaturals.com

TUSCAN SUN-DRIED TOMATO PESTO

Yield approximately 1 cup

I continuously get awesome reviews for this outstanding recipe. I like taking it as a dish to pass when I visit friends, along with vegetable crudite and/or flax crackers.

1 cup sun-dried tomatoes, soaked 2 hours in enough water just to cover, reserve soak water

1/2 cup fresh basil, packed

(continued)

1/4 cup pine nuts

1 teaspoon garlic, pressed

1 teaspoon Himalayan crystal salt

2 tablespoons fresh lemon juice

1/3 cup extra virgin olive oil

Combine all of the ingredients, except the olive oil, in a food processor, fitted with the "S" blade, adding a smidge of the soak water, if necessary. While the mixture is pureeing, add the olive oil.

Serving suggestions:

- Toss this with some zucchini angel hair pasta for a truly satisfying meal
- Stuff inside turnip Rawvioli and eat in style
- Place 1/4 cup (or more!) of this wonderful pate on top of a salad for a truly satisfying entree
- Roll in a collard green with some fresh chopped veggies for an awesome sandwich to fill even the hungriest of tummies
- Serve with sliced cucumbers or zucchini

MOROCCAN PESTO-N-PASTA

Yield 4 servings

The Pasta

4 - 6 carrots

The Pesto

 1 cup fresh cilantro, tightly packed

 1 cup fresh parsley, tightly packed

 1/2 cup fresh mint, chopped

 2 cloves garlic, pressed

 1/4 teaspoon cumin

 1/2 teaspoon Himalayan crystal salt

 1/4 cup extra virgin olive oil

 1/3 cup macadamia nuts, chopped

To make the pesto, place the cilantro, parsley, mint, garlic, cumin and salt in a food processor, fitted with the "S" blade, and process until the cilantro and mint are chopped. While the food processor is running, add the olive oil. Then, add the chopped macadamia nuts and process until fairly smooth. Stored in a sealed container in the refrigerator, Moroccan Pesto will keep for up to five days.

To make the pasta, use a spiralizer or turning slicer to make angel hair or linguini style noodles with the carrots (or use beets). Toss the carrots with enough pesto to coat.

"TAKE ME TO INDIA" PESTO-N-RICE

Yield 4 servings

The Pesto

 2 cups spinach, packed

(continued)

1/4 cup extra virgin olive oil

1 tablespoon fresh lime juice (or lemon)

2 cloves garlic, pressed

1 1/2 teaspoons Himalayan crystal salt

1 teaspoon curry powder

1/4 teaspoon cardamom

1/3 cup pine nuts

To make the pesto, place the spinach, olive oil, lime juice, garlic, salt, curry and cardamom in a food processor, fitted with the "S" blade and process until chopped. Add the pine nuts and process until smooth. Stored in a sealed container in the refrigerator, the pesto will keep for 4 - 5 days.

The Rice

1 head cauliflower, florets

1/4 cup pine nuts

3 tablespoons fresh orange juice

1 tablespoon fresh lemon juice

1 tablespoon agave nectar

1/2 teaspoon cinnamon

Place the cauliflower and pine nuts in a food processor, fitted with the "S" blade, and pulse until chopped to the approximate size of rice. You might need to do this in more than one batch. Set this aside in a bowl. Take the remaining ingredients and whisk together in a bowl. Pour over the rice ingredients and toss to mix. Serve as is, topped with pesto, or take the rice another step. You can spread the rice mixture on a dehydrator paraflex sheet at 140 degrees for about 1 - 1 1/2 hours. Transfer to a plate and top with pesto.

HEARTY GARDEN BURGERS

See photo at KristensRaw.com/photos.

Yield 6 - 8 servings

Whooo-heee, these are so good. In fact, the last time I taught this recipe in class a woman said out loud, "This is a WOW DAY!" She wasn't even my mother. ☺

    1/2 cup pecans or walnuts

    1/4 cup sunflower seeds

    1/4 cup hemp seeds

    1/2 cup chia meal (or flax meal)

    1/3 cup sun-dried tomatoes, soaked 1 hour, drained
    and sliced

    1 tablespoon ginger, peeled and minced

    2 cloves fresh garlic, pressed

    1 teaspoon Himalayan crystal salt

    2 - 3 carrots, chopped

    1 stalk celery, chopped

    1/2 cup red or yellow bell pepper, stemmed, seeded
    and chopped

    1/2 cup zucchini, chopped

    1/4 yellow or red onion, chopped

    1 tablespoon fresh lemon juice or lime juice

    1 tablespoon water

    1/2 cup dates, pitted, and chopped

Process the pecans and sunflower seeds into a fine grind using a food processor, fitted with the "S" blade. Add the hemp seeds and pulse to thoroughly mix. Set aside in a large bowl.

Add the chia (or flax) meal to the ground nut/seed mixture and stir to mix.

Process the sun-dried tomatoes, ginger, garlic, and salt in the food processor. Add the carrots, celery, red bell pepper, zucchini, onion, lemon juice and water and process. Don't process too much or it gets mushy. Transfer this vegetable mix to the bowl with the ground nut/seed mixture. Add the dates. Toss briefly to incorporate.

Take 1/3 - 1/2 of the mixture and place back in the food processor and pulse a few times to mix. Transfer to a new bowl. Repeat that process until you've done that with all of the mixture.

Form 1/3-cup patties and enjoy on a crisp lettuce leaf as your bun. Or for a more gourmet bun, use two slices of Raw bread (see Chapter 3 for recipes).

Optional and recommended steps:

- These are delicious plain or you can add some sensational *Raw Mustard* (see recipe p. 26) and *Raw Savory Sweet Ketchup* (see recipe, below) so you have all the fixins. ☺
- Dehydrate the patties at 140 degrees for 1 hour. Lower the temperature to 105 degrees and dehydrate for another 4 - 8 hours or more, depending on how "dry" you want them. Enjoy!

Variation:

- Replace the sunflower seeds with black sesame seeds (and use chia instead of flax) to make a burger that has a darker color, more reminiscent of a meat burger

Additional serving suggestions:

- Roll these into fresh garden "meat" balls and enjoy them with zucchini pasta marinara
- Stuff the pate into a half of a seeded, orange bell pepper or a tomato. Fantastic!

Raw Savory Sweet Ketchup

Yield 2 1/2 cups

3/4 cup fresh tomatoes, chopped

1 cup sun-dried tomatoes, soaked 1 hour in just enough water to cover, reserve soak water

1 tablespoon apple cider vinegar

2 cloves garlic

2 1/2 teaspoons ginger, peeled and grated

2 - 3 dates, pitted (or 2 tablespoons raisins)

3 - 4 tablespoons raw agave nectar

2 tablespoons extra virgin olive oil

1 teaspoon onion powder

1 teaspoon Himalayan crystal salt

pinch black pepper

1 - 2 tablespoons of water, if needed

Blend all of the ingredients, including the tomato soak water, until smooth. Ketchup will last up to one week stored in a glass jar in the refrigerator.

ISLAND COCONUT BURGERS

Yield 6 - 10 burgers

Your family is sure to love these! If it's just for you, no worries... make them and freeze the leftovers.

1 3/4 cups carrot pulp*

3 tablespoons dried pineapple, ground**

1 1/2 cups young Thai coconut meat

1/2 cup young Thai coconut water (more if needed)

2 tablespoons fresh lime juice

3 tablespoons black tahini

1 tablespoon tamari, wheat-free or 1 teaspoon Himalayan crystal salt

1 teaspoon fresh ginger, peeled and grated

2 cloves garlic, pressed

2 tablespoons fresh cilantro, chopped

1 tablespoon fresh mint, minced

1/2 cup flax meal (or chia meal)

Place the carrot pulp in a large bowl. In a food processor, fitted with the "S" blade, combine the ground dried pineapple, coconut meat, coconut water, lime juice, tahini, tamari, ginger, and garlic. Once it's combined, add the cilantro and mint, and pulse to mix. Add the coconut mixture to the bowl with the carrot pulp. Mix by hand. Add the flax meal and mix to incorporate everything with your hands.

Form 1/3-cup patties and eat as is (wrapped in a lettuce leaf as your bun), or dehydrate at 140 degrees for 1 hour. Lower the temperature to 105 degrees and continue dehydrating another 4 - 6 hours, or longer.

* To get carrot pulp, juice carrots until you have about 1 3/4 cups of pulp. Set aside in a large bowl.
** To grind the dried pineapple, use a food processor, fitted with the "S" blade.

Serving suggestion:

- Instead of eating on lettuce, serve "the meat" as a pate stuffed into half of a seeded, orange bell pepper or a tomato. Fantastic!

NUTTY BUTTER AND SWEET BERRY JAM SANDWICH ON CHOCOLATE BREAD

Yield 1 serving

Spread some of this creamy nut butter and jam between two slices of chocolate bread and serve alongside a sliced banana for a fun meal. Now, what kid doesn't want to take this to school for lunch?

2 tablespoons raw nut (or seed) butter

1 teaspoon raw agave nectar

2 pieces of *Chocolate Snack Bread* (see recipe, p. 87)

3 tablespoons *Sweet Berry Jam* (see recipe, below)

Mix the almond butter with the agave in a bowl. Spread this on one slice of the chocolate bread. Spread the *Sweet Berry Jam* on the other slice of bread. Enjoy.

The Sweet Berry Jam

Yield approximately 1 1/4 cups

1 1/2 cups fresh berries

6 soft dates, pitted, chopped

Blend up the berries. Add the dates and pulse to thoroughly incorporate.

KRISTEN SUZANNE'S RAW ITALIAN MIX

Yield 1/2 cup

This delicious Italian Mix is great to have on hand for adding tons of flavor to any meal. It takes a little longer than some other recipes, but it's worth it. Trust me! You'll be coming back for more.

2 tablespoons FRESH basil, minced

2 tablespoons FRESH parsley, chopped

2 tablespoons FRESH garlic, minced

2 teaspoons dried thyme

2 teaspoons dried oregano

2 teaspoons ground black pepper

1 teaspoon FRESH rosemary, minced

1 teaspoon Himalayan crystal salt

1/4 teaspoon cayenne pepper

1 tablespoon extra virgin olive oil

1/2 teaspoon fresh lemon juice

Combine all of the ingredients in a small glass mason jar and stir or shake to incorporate. Store in the refrigerator for up to three days.

Serving suggestions:

• Toss it on your salads

- Use as a dip with a few tablespoons of olive or hemp oil for your Raw crackers or bread
- Add it into a veggie smoothie to kick it up a notch!
- Use it to make an extra flavorful Raw vegan soup

ON-THE-GO RAW CHEESE

Yield 1 cup

This is a great cheese you can make on-the-go for use in a number of entrees. It doesn't require any soaking or fermenting. Just whip it up in the blender or food processor and enjoy.

This cheese can be spread on big crunchy flax crackers for a delicious and fulfilling cheese sandwich or you can use it as a dip for veggies and/or fruit to have a satisfying meal. I also love using this quick cheese recipe spread inside my collard green sandwich wraps.

1 cup Brazil nuts, unsoaked

3 - 4 tablespoons water, more if necessary

2 tablespoons fresh lemon juice

2 tablespoons tamari, wheat-free*

1 tablespoon coconut oil

1 - 2 cloves garlic

2 teaspoons nutritional yeast (optional, but definitely adds a "cheesier" flavor)

Blend all of the ingredients, adding more water to help keep the cheese blending. Voila! You're done!

* If you're trying to watch your sodium intake, reduce the tamari to only 1 tablespoon and increase the nutritional yeast

to 1 or 2 tablespoons, while increasing the water to make sure it's blending for you.

HIGH ENERGY BANANA-ROMAINE SANDWICH

Yield 1 sandwich

This is so super duper easy, refreshing, and shockingly good. Make two of them for an extra satisfying meal (breakfast, lunch, or dinner!).

    1 large romaine leaf or collard green
    1 large banana, peeled

Wrap your banana in the romaine and chomp away.

Variation:

- Want to make it extra filling or want to add some protein to it? Simply spread 1 tablespoon of raw almond butter, hemp butter or raw tahini on it AND/OR sprinkle the banana with hemp seeds.

NO PIGS IN THIS BLANKET

Yield 4 servings

You can make your own sauerkraut for this recipe, or you can buy a jar at the health food store. One of my favorite brands is Rejuvenative®.

1 cup sauerkraut

2 tablespoons *Raw Mustard**, or more to taste

8 romaine lettuce leaves

2 cups *Simple Sun-Dried Tomato Pate* (see recipe, below)

In a bowl, mix the sauerkraut and mustard together. Place 1/4-cup oblong-shaped patties of *Simple Sun-Dried Tomato Pate* on top of each romaine lettuce. Spread 2 tablespoons of the sauerkraut mixture on top of each one. Roll up like a blanket and gobble them up!

* See recipe for *Raw Mustard* (p. 26). If you don't have *Raw Mustard* already made, then don't let that stop you from making this wonderful dish. Although not Raw, you can just substitute regular mustard from a bottle.

SIMPLE SUN-DRIED TOMATO PATE

Yield 2 1/2 cups

1 1/2 cups macadamia nuts, pine nuts, or hemp seeds

1/4 teaspoon Himalayan crystal salt, or more to taste

pinch black pepper

1 1/2 cups sun-dried tomatoes, soaked 1 hour with enough water to just cover, reserve soak water

2 cloves garlic, pressed

10 fresh basil leaves

Place the nuts, salt, and pepper in a food processor, fitted with the "S" blade, and process until coarsely ground. Add the sun-dried tomatoes, soak water, and garlic and process until thoroughly mixed like a pate. Add the basil leaves and pulse briefly to mix. Add more water if necessary to get the mixture going.

Simple Sun-Dried Tomato Pate will last up to five days in an airtight container in the refrigerator. It also freezes well.

Serving suggestions:

- Place 1/4 cup of this wonderful pate on top of a salad for a truly satisfying entree
- Stuff in a seeded orange or red bell pepper and enjoy both a fresh crunch from the bell pepper and nice chewiness from the pate for a delicious dinner
- Stuff in half of a seeded tomato or two
- Roll in a collard green with some fresh chopped veggies for an awesome sandwich to fill even the hungriest of tummies
- Serve on top of zucchini angel hair pasta (try rolling them into balls to serve as hearty "meat" balls and add *Kristen Suzanne's Famous Marinara* – see p. 50)
- For a real satisfying meal, form 1/4 cup patties and dehydrate at 140 degrees for 1 hour. Lower the temperature and continue dehydrating another 4 - 6 hours. Eat warm right out of the dehydrator or freeze for use later

SOUTH OF THE BORDER BURRITO

See photo at KristensRaw.com/photos.

Yield 2 1/2 cups

Wow, I love this recipe when I'm craving a good ol' satisfying bean burrito (as shown in the picture) topped with chopped tomatoes or *Fresh Salsa* (see recipe, p. 67) and *Cheezy Nacho Sauce!* (see recipe, p. 67).

3/4 cup sunflower seeds

3/4 cup pumpkin seeds, soaked 6 hours, drained and rinsed

1/4 teaspoon Himalayan crystal salt, or more to taste

pinch black pepper

3/4 cup sun-dried tomatoes, soaked 1 hour with enough water to just cover, reserve the soak water

2 cloves garlic, pressed

1 tablespoon fresh lime juice

1 1/2 teaspoons chili powder

1 teaspoon cumin

1 teaspoon dark miso

1 teaspoon onion powder

1/4 cup fresh cilantro, chopped

water, if needed (see instructions)

Grind the sunflower seeds into a fine grind, using a food processor, fitted with the "S" blade. Add the soaked pumpkin seeds, salt, pepper, sun-dried tomatoes, soak water, garlic, lime juice, chili powder, cumin, dark miso, and onion powder, and process until thoroughly mixed like a pate. Add more water in this process, if necessary to get the mixture going. Add the cilantro and pulse briefly to mix. This pate will last up to five days in an airtight container in the refrigerator. It also freezes well.

Variations:

- Place 1/4 cup of this Mexican flavored pate on top of a salad for an entrée that is both refreshing and comforting
- Stuff in a seeded orange or red bell pepper and enjoy both a fresh crunch from the bell pepper and nice chewiness from the pate for a delicious dinner
- Stuff in half of a seeded tomato or two
- Roll in a collard green with some fresh chopped veggies for an awesome sandwich to fill even the hungriest of tummies
- Serve on top of zucchini angel hair pasta (try rolling into balls to serve as hearty "meat" balls and top with *Fresh Salsa* – see recipe, p. 67 – or chopped tomatoes)
- For a real satisfying meal, form 1/4 cup patties and dehydrate at 140 degrees for 1 hour. Lower the temperature and continue dehydrating another 4 - 6 hours. Eat warm right out of the dehydrator or freeze for use later

SUN-DRENCHED ITALY PATE

Yield approximately 3 1/2 cups

The combination of flavors (fennel, basil, oregano, sun-dried tomatoes, and rosemary) take my mind on a trip to Italy, *and I don't want to come back.* ☺

1 cup sunflower seeds, soaked 6 hours, drained and rinsed

1/2 cup almonds, soaked 8 - 12 hours, drained and rinsed

(continued)

3/4 cup sun-dried tomatoes, soaked 1 hour, drained and slivered (keep soak water)

1/4 cup sun-dried tomato powder*

1 1/2 tablespoons fresh lemon juice

2 teaspoons light miso

1 tablespoon tamari, wheat-free, or to taste

1 teaspoon fennel seed, ground

2 cloves garlic, pressed

1 teaspoon black pepper

1/4 cup fresh basil, chopped, or 1 tablespoon dried

2 teaspoons fresh oregano or 1/2 teaspoon dried

1 tablespoon fresh rosemary leaves, chopped, or 1 teaspoon dried

Place all of the ingredients, except the basil, oregano and rosemary, in a food processor fitted with the "S" blade, and process until you get a pate quality, adding some of the soak water from the sun-dried tomatoes, if necessary. Add the basil, oregano and rosemary and pulse until mixed.

Variations:

- Add other herbs such as parsley, thyme or sage
- Use different nuts and seeds

Serving suggestions:

- Serve 1/4 cup of the pate on top of a lovely salad
- Stuff in half of a seeded orange or red bell pepper or stuffed in half of a tomato – this is a fabulous meal
- Roll in a collard green (or a big leaf of romaine lettuce) with some fresh chopped veggies for a great sandwich
- Serve with a plate full of vegetables for a hearty meal

- Roll this into nice big "meat" balls and add to zucchini pasta marinara
- Eat these like a burger by forming 1/4-cup patties and dehydrate at 140 degrees for one hour. Lower the temperature and continue dehydrating another 4 - 6 hours. Eat warm right out of the dehydrator or freeze for use later
- Use as the stuffing for Rawvioli

* To make the sun-dried tomato powder, grind 1 cup of sun-dried tomatoes in a dry blender. Store in a glass mason jar in your refrigerator. This is always good to have on hand and makes a great addition to almost any salad dressing, sauce or soup. One cup of sun-dried tomatoes yields about 2/3 - 3/4 cup powder.

KRISTEN SUZANNE'S FAMOUS MARINARA WITH PASTA

Yield approximately 3 cups / 6 servings

Your out of town guests will love this. In fact, they won't want to leave your house. Hmmm. On second thought, you might not want to make this for them.

The Sauce

4 - 5 medium tomatoes, cut in quarters (seed 3 of them)

1 cup sun-dried tomatoes, soaked 1hour, drained and chopped

(continued)

50

1/3 cup yellow or red onion, chopped

1/4 cup fresh basil

2 tablespoons apple cider vinegar

2 tablespoons tamari, wheat free

2 tablespoons extra virgin olive oil

2 tablespoons fresh oregano, chopped (or 2 teaspoons dried)

1 clove garlic

1 tablespoon Italian Seasoning

5 kalamata olives, pitted and chopped

The Pasta

5 zucchini or carrots, spiralized or peeled with a vegetable peeler

Place all of the sauce ingredients in a food processor, fitted with the "S" blade (or a blender) and pulse until combined. Don't process too long; the sauce is best when it's chunky. Serve this on top of any veggie pasta and you'll think you're in heaven.

Variation:

- Celery root and beets make fantastic noodles

MARINARA #2 (fat-free) WITH ZUCCHINI PASTA

Yield approximately 3 cups / 6 servings

This is another great marinara and it's fat free, too.

The Sauce

4 medium size tomatoes, chopped

1/2 cup sun-dried tomatoes, soaked 1hour, drained and chopped

1/4 cup sun-dried tomato powder*

1/4 cup fennel, chopped

3 tablespoons red onion, chopped

1/4 cup fresh basil

1 clove garlic

2 teaspoons fresh lemon juice

1 tablespoon Italian seasoning

1 1/2 teaspoons dried oregano

1/2 - 3/4 teaspoon Himalayan crystal salt

1/4 - 1/2 teaspoon black pepper

pinch cinnamon

The Pasta

5 zucchini or carrots, spiralized or peeled with a vegetable peeler.

Place all of the sauce ingredients in a food processor, fitted with the "S" blade (or a blender) and pulse until combined. Don't process too long; the sauce is best when it's chunky. Serve on top of zucchini or any other vegetable noodles.

Variation:

• Celery root and beets make fantastic noodles

* To make the sun-dried tomato powder, grind dry sun-dried tomatoes in a dry blender or coffee grinder until you get a powder. Store in a glass mason jar in your refrigerator. It's always good to have this on hand. It makes a great addition to almost any salad dressing, sauce or soup. One cup of sun-dried tomatoes yields about 2/3 - 3/4 cup powder.

NO-MEAT RAWVIOLI

Yield 4 servings (6 Rawvioli per person)

The Noodle

> 1 - 2 large parsnips, turnips, celery roots, beets (golden or red), or jicama, sliced into very thin rounds with a V-slicer or mandoline *
>
> 1/2 cup extra virgin olive oil (or more)
>
> 1 1/2 tablespoons Himalayan crystal salt (or more)
>
> 2 tablespoons fresh lemon juice (or more)

Place the sliced vegetable rounds (or squares) into a shallow baking dish with the olive oil, salt and lemon juice to marinate for 15 - 20 minutes. Optional step: Briefly rinse under water to remove some of the salt and oil.

* You'll want about 24 slices of vegetable if you're going to present the dish using 1 slice of vegetable per Rawvioli (folding them in 1/2 for a half moon shape or triangle). Or, you'll need 48 slices of vegetable if you're using 2 slices per Rawvioli (1 on top of the other for a full moon shape or square).

The No-Meat Filling

1 cup macadamia nuts or hemp seeds

2 cloves garlic, pressed

pinch black pepper

1 cup sun-dried tomatoes, soaked 1 hour with enough water to just cover, reserve the soak water

1 tablespoon fresh lemon juice

2 teaspoons tamari, wheat-free

1/4 cup fresh basil leaves, chopped or 1 1/4 tablespoons dried

2 tablespoons fresh oregano, chopped or 2 teaspoons dried

1 green onion sliced (white and green parts)

Place the nuts, garlic, and pepper in a food processor, fitted with the "S" blade, and process until coarsely ground. Add the sun-dried tomatoes, soak water, lemon juice, and tamari and process until thoroughly mixed like a pate. Add the basil, oregano, and green onion and pulse briefly to mix. This freezes well.

The Rawvioli Assembly

Take one slice of vegetable round at a time and put approximately 1 teaspoon of filling onto it. You can fold over the Rawvioli (like a half moon) or lay it flat on the serving plate while placing another slice of vegetable round on top. You can store any leftover filling in an airtight container in the refrigerator for up to 5 days.

Serving suggestions:

- Serve plain or garnished with some fresh (or dried) herbs
- Serve them slathered in *Kristen Suzanne's Famous Marinara* (see p. 50)

CHEEZY RAWVIOLI

See photo at KristensRaw.com/photos.

Yield 4 servings (6 Rawvioli per person)

Rawvioli is one of my favorite meals to make. They're full of flavor and completely satisfying.

The Noodle

> 1 - 2 large parsnips, celery roots, turnips, beets (golden or red), or jicama, sliced into very thin rounds with a V-slicer or mandoline *
>
> 1/2 cup extra virgin olive oil (or more)
>
> 1 1/2 tablespoons Himalayan crystal salt (or more)
>
> 2 tablespoons fresh lemon juice (or more)

Place the sliced vegetable rounds (or squares) into a shallow baking dish with the olive oil, salt and lemon juice to marinate for 15 - 20 minutes. Optional step: Briefly rinse under water to remove some of the salt and oil.

* You'll want about 24 slices of vegetable if you're going to present the dish using 1 slice of vegetable per Rawvioli (folding them in 1/2 for a half moon shape or triangle). Or, you'll need 48 slices of vegetable if you're using 2 slices per Rawvioli (1 on top of the other for a full moon shape or square).

The Cheeze Filling

1 cup pine nuts, soaked 1 hour, drained and rinsed

2 - 4 tablespoons water, more if necessary

2 tablespoons fresh lemon juice

1 1/2 tablespoons tamari, wheat-free

1 large clove garlic

2 teaspoons nutritional yeast

1 teaspoon dried thyme or rosemary

Blend all of the ingredients, adding more water to help keep the cheese blending, if necessary (but keep it thick).

The Rawvioli Assembly

Take one slice of vegetable round at a time and put approximately 1 teaspoon of cheese filling onto it. You can fold over the Rawvioli (like a half moon) or lay it flat on the serving plate and place another slice of vegetable round on top. Store leftover cheese in an airtight container in the refrigerator for up to 5 days.

Serving suggestions:

- Serve plain or garnished with some fresh (or dried) herbs
- Serve with *Kristen Suzanne's Famous Marinara* (see p. 50) poured on top of the Rawvioli

KRISTEN SUZANNE'S ITALIAN LASAGNA

See photo on cover and at KristensRaw.com/photos.

Yield one 7 x 7 glass baking dish or spring form pan

The Noodles

2 - 3 zucchini, sliced into 1/16 inch thick rounds

Place the zucchini rounds on a mesh dehydrator tray and dehydrate at 105 degrees for 45 minutes.

The Marinara

7 - 8 tomatoes, seeded and quartered (about 7 cups)

3/4 cup sun-dried tomato powder*

1/3 cup yellow or red onion, chopped

2 cloves garlic, pressed

1 tablespoon Italian seasoning

5 kalamata olives, pitted and sliced

1 tablespoon apple cider vinegar, or fresh lemon juice

1 tablespoon tamari, wheat free

1/4 cup fresh basil, chopped

2 tablespoons fresh oregano, chopped, or 2 teaspoons dried

Place the tomatoes in a food processor, fitted with the "S" blade, and briefly pulse (keep it chunky). Add the sun-dried tomato powder, onion, garlic, Italian seasoning, olives, apple cider vinegar, and tamari and pulse briefly to incorporate. Add the basil and oregano and pulse to mix briefly. Place the marinara in a fine mesh strainer, over a bowl, to drain off any excess water while you prepare the remaining components to the lasagna. You don't want marinara that's too "wet" or it will have trouble holding together in the lasagna.

* To make the sun-dried tomato powder, grind 1 cup of sun-dried tomatoes in a dry blender. Store in a glass mason jar in your refrigerator. This is always good to have on hand and makes a great addition to almost any salad dressing, sauce or soup. One cup of sun-dried tomatoes yields about 2/3 - 3/4 cup powder.

The Mushrooms (optional)

> 20 mushrooms, sliced
> 1 1/2 teaspoons tamari, wheat-free
> 2 tablespoons hemp oil or olive oil
> 1 teaspoon fresh lemon juice
> pinch of black pepper

Toss the mushrooms in the tamari, oil, lemon juice, and pepper. Set aside for at least 10 minutes to marinate. Drain well and gently squeeze to remove excess liquid.

The Ricotta Cheeze

> 2 cups Brazil nuts
> 1 clove garlic, more if you like
> 2 1/2 teaspoons nutritional yeast
> 2 teaspoons tamari, wheat-free
> dash nutmeg
> pinch black pepper

Using a food process, fitted with the "S" blade, process all of the ingredients until it's a thick puree (you may add a little water, if needed). Voila! You're done with the cheeze!

The Spinach

1 bunch spinach

1 teaspoon dried basil

Briefly chop the spinach and dried basil in a food processor, fitted with the "S" blade, and set aside.

The Assembly

Spread a thin, sparse layer of the marinara on the bottom of a 7 x 7 glass-baking dish or spring form pan (my favorite because it's easier to cut out of this kind of pan). Place a layer of zucchini on top of the sparse layer of marinara (don't overlap the zucchini).

Spread another layer of the marinara over the zucchini, making it a little thicker this time. Then spread a layer of the mushroom mixture and press gently (if using). Place a layer of the cheeze on top of that, followed by a layer of the spinach mixture and continue layering: zucchini, marinara, mushrooms, cheeze, and spinach. Press gently, but firmly, between each layer.

Keep layering until you get to the top of your pan or until you run out of lasagna components. It's easiest to do this process using a small offset spatula.

Serve immediately at room temperature or warmed slightly in the dehydrator set at 135 degrees for 1 - 2 hours. Store in an airtight container in the refrigerator for up to three days.

Leftover components:

- Sometimes I have some leftovers of the different components of the lasagna that didn't fit into the spring-form pan. When this happens, I stir it all up in a bowl and eat it like goulash! Yum!

BASIL MY BROCCOLI (OR ANY VEGGIES!)

Yield 1-cup oil to put on as many veggies as you can

This is a great sauce that's super simple to make. It immediately transforms any veggies into a delightful meal. If you're looking for an easier way to get veggies down, look no further because this is it!

1 head broccoli florets, chopped

The Herb Oil

1 nice size bunch (1 - 2 big handfuls) of fresh basil or any fresh herb

1 - 2 cloves garlic (depending on how much you like garlic!)

2 - 3 pinches Himalayan crystal salt

pinch black pepper

pinch cayenne, optional

1 cup extra virgin olive oil or hemp oil

The Veggies

Any veggies are perfect for this. For the purposes of this recipe, I'm using broccoli because I don't like broccoli by itself. This is one way I can easily get more broccoli in my diet... by eating it with this delicious gourmet herb oil.

Process the basil, garlic, salt, pepper and cayenne in a food processor until finely chopped. While the food processor is running, slowly add the olive oil. Drizzle the oil mixture on your vegetables or use as a dipping sauce. Enjoy!

HURRY MY CURRY VEGETABLES

People email me all the time telling me how much they love this entree.

Yield 2 servings

The Vegetables

2 tomatoes, diced

2 zucchini, diced

2 carrots, diced

2 tablespoons onion, minced

fresh corn from 1 cob, if available

The Sauce

2 tablespoons water

(continued)

1/4 cup coconut oil

2 tablespoons fresh lime juice

1 - 2 cloves garlic, pressed

1 teaspoon fresh ginger, peeled and grated

1 teaspoon curry powder

1/2 red Serrano pepper, seeded and finely chopped

1/4 teaspoon fresh lime zest

1 teaspoon cumin

1/4 teaspoon Himalayan crystal salt

1/4 cup fresh cilantro, finely chopped

Place the chopped vegetables in a bowl and set aside. Then, place the water, coconut oil, lime juice, garlic, ginger, curry, Serrano pepper, lime zest, cumin and salt in a bowl and whisk together. Stir in the cilantro. Pour this yummy sauce over vegetables and eat.

NO-VODKA SAUCE WITH ZUCCHINI PASTA

See photo at KristensRaw.com/photos.

Yield 4 servings

You can eat this on top of spiralized vegetable noodles, chopped veggies or eat it as a chunky stew. Whichever way you choose, it's a delicious entree.

The Sauce

4 medium size tomatoes, cut in half (seed 3 of them)

3/4 cup sun-dried tomatoes, soaked 1 hour, drained and chopped

1/2 cup raw tahini

1/3 cup yellow or red onion, chopped

3 tablespoons fresh basil, chopped or 1 tablespoon dried

2 tablespoons fresh lime juice

2 tablespoons tamari, wheat free

1 tablespoon apple cider vinegar

1 clove garlic

5 kalamata olives, pitted and sliced, optional

1 teaspoon dried oregano

1/2 teaspoon cayenne, to taste

black pepper, to taste

pinch Himalayan crystal salt, to taste

The Pasta

5 - 6 zucchini or carrots, spiralized into angel hair pasta or peeled like fettuccini with a vegetable peeler

Briefly process all of the sauce ingredients together in a food processor, fitted with the "S" blade. (I prefer this to be fairly chunky.) Serve on top of the fresh spiralized zucchini pasta or a mix of other chopped vegetables.

AMALFI COAST PIZZA

See photo at KristensRaw.com/photos.

Yield 2 servings

The 2 pizza crusts

 1 cup sunflower seeds, ground
 1/2 tablespoon flax meal
 1 stalk celery
 3 - 4 tablespoons water
 1 1/2 teaspoons extra virgin olive oil
 1/2 teaspoon fresh lemon zest
 pinch cinnamon
 pinch Himalayan crystal salt

Combine the ground sunflower seeds and flax meal in a bowl and set aside. Blend the celery, water, oil, lemon zest, cinnamon and salt in a blender. Transfer the blended mixture to the bowl with ground seeds and stir or mix with your hands.

Form the crusts by dividing the mixture in half and spreading it into rounds with an offset spatula, onto a paraflex dehydrator sheet until it's about 1/4-inch thick. Dehydrate at 140 degrees for 1 hour. Lower the temperature to 105 degrees and continue dehydrating another 5 - 6 hours. Flip the crusts onto their other side, onto the *mesh* dehydrator sheet and keep dehydrating for 5 - 8 more hours, until dry.

The Toppings

1/2 cup *Kristen Suzanne's Famous Marinara* (see p. 50)

4 mushrooms, cleaned and sliced, optional

The Cheeze

1/2 cup pine nuts, soaked 1 hour, drained and rinsed

2 tablespoons water, more if necessary

1 tablespoon fresh lemon juice

1 tablespoon tamari, wheat-free*

1 clove garlic, more if you like

1 teaspoon nutritional yeast

Blend all of the ingredients, adding a little more water to help keep the cheese blending if needed.

* If you're watching your sodium intake, you can reduce the amount of tamari and add another teaspoon of nutritional yeast to make sure you get a cheeze flavor.

The Assembly

Spread some of the cheeze on top of each crust, followed by 3 - 4 tablespoons of the marinara, topped with sliced mushrooms. Serve immediately. Store any leftover components in airtight containers in the refrigerator.

MEXICAN FIESTA PIZZA

Yield 2 servings

The 2 pizza crusts

1 cup pumpkin seeds, ground
1/2 tablespoon ground flax meal
1 stalk celery
3 - 4 tablespoons water
1 1/2 teaspoons extra virgin olive oil
1/2 teaspoon fresh lime zest
dash cumin
pinch Himalayan crystal salt

Combine the ground pumpkin seeds and flax meal in a bowl and set aside. Blend the celery, water, oil, lime zest, cumin and salt in a blender. Transfer the blended mixture to the bowl with ground seeds and stir or mix with your hands.

Form the crusts by dividing the mixture in half and spreading it into rounds using an offset spatula, onto a paraflex dehydrator sheet until it's about 1/4-inch thick. Dehydrate at 140 degrees for one hour. Lower the temperature to 105 degrees and continue dehydrating another 5 - 6 hours. Flip the crusts onto their other side, onto the *mesh* dehydrator sheet and continue dehydrating for 5 - 8 more hours, until dry.

The Toppings

1 avocado, pitted, peeled, and sliced

The Cheezy Nacho Sauce

1/4 cup pine nuts, soaked 1 hour, drained and rinsed

1/4 cup sunflower seeds, soaked 6 hours, drained and rinsed

2 - 3 tablespoons water*

1/2 red bell pepper, stemmed, seeded and chopped

1 small carrot, chopped

1 clove garlic

1 tablespoon nutritional yeast

1 tablespoon fresh lemon juice or lime juice

1/2 teaspoon Himalayan crystal salt

1/8 - 1/4 teaspoon cayenne pepper, more or less depending on how spicy you like it

1 teaspoon Mexican seasoning

Put all of the ingredients in a blender and blend until smooth and creamy*.

* Add more water if necessary to achieve creamy texture.

The Fresh Salsa

3 - 4 medium tomatoes, seeded and diced

1 green onion, thinly sliced

1 clove garlic, pressed

2 tablespoons fresh cilantro, minced

1 tablespoon fresh lime juice

pinch Himalayan crystal salt

pinch cayenne pepper

Combine all of the ingredients together in a bowl and toss briefly.

The Assembly

Spread some of the cheeze on top of each pizza crust, followed by some of the fresh salsa and then top each pizza with avocado slices. Serve immediately. Store any leftover components in airtight containers in the refrigerator.

EXQUISITE CILANTRO GINGER PESTO

Yield approximately 2 cups

This fabulous variation of traditional pesto will blow your mind. It's fantastic and so healthy for you, too!

1 bunch fresh parsley, chopped

1 bunch fresh cilantro, chopped

1/2 cup pine nuts

1 - 2 Serrano red peppers, whole (stem removed)

3 tablespoons raw agave nectar

3 tablespoons fresh ginger, peeled, grated

1 - 1 1/2 teaspoons Himalayan crystal salt

1/8 teaspoon black pepper

1 cup extra virgin olive oil

In your food processor, fitted with the "S" blade, process all of the ingredients except the olive oil. While the food processor is still running, slowly add the olive oil. Store in an airtight container until ready to use.

Serving suggestions:

- Scoop some of this yummy pesto into lettuce cups for a delicious meal
- Gobble it up with fresh vegetable crudite
- Serve on top of vegetable noodles for a unique pasta dish
- Toss 1/4 - 1/2 cup with 1 cup of shredded carrots
- Stuff into half of a seeded orange, yellow, or red bell pepper

INDIAN MARINARA ENTREE

Yield 4 - 6 servings / 3 cups

This is definitely one of my favorite entrees (my husband's, too!). The delicate Indian flavor makes it deliciously unique.

The Sauce

2 orange or red bell peppers, stemmed, seeded and chopped

1 medium tomato, chopped

1/2 cup sun-dried tomatoes, soaked 1 hour and drained

2 tablespoons extra virgin olive oil

1 tablespoon apple cider vinegar

1 tablespoon curry powder

1 clove garlic

(continued)

1 teaspoon fresh ginger, peeled and grated

1 teaspoon Himalayan crystal salt

3/4 teaspoon cumin

1/4 teaspoon cinnamon

2 cloves, crushed

pinch cayenne pepper

pinch cardamom

The Noodles

4 - 5 zucchini or carrots, chopped into chunks or spiralized into noodles

Blend all of the sauce ingredients together. Place the zucchini or carrots into a bowl and pour the Indian Marinara on top.

Alternate serving suggestion:

- You can serve this with a variety of chopped vegetables and eat it right out of a bowl, like a stew, and dip crispy flax crackers in it

CARIBBEAN JERKY

Yield 1 serving

This is scrumptious and so satisfying! It's really easy to make, too. This recipe is for one serving, so make sure to double or triple it if you're really hungry or having company.

1/2 cup young Thai coconut meat, sliced into noodles, packed

1/2 teaspoon poppy seeds

3/4 teaspoon coconut oil

1/2 teaspoon curry powder

1/4 teaspoon ground ginger

1/4 teaspoon allspice

1/4 teaspoon vanilla extract

pinch Himalayan crystal salt

pinch cayenne

Toss all of the ingredients together well. Dehydrate at 140 degrees for one hour on a mesh dehydrator sheet. Lower the temperature to 105 degrees and dehydrate another 2 - 4 hours.

LEFT-OVER WRAPPED LUNCH

Yield 1 serving

This is one of the easiest meals you can make because you're essentially just using leftovers, not to mention one of the most flavor-filled. It's a win-win every time!

1 collard green

2 tablespoons of any left over cheese spread, dressing, or pate you have in your refrigerator

1 handful alfalfa, sunflower and/or pea sprouts

1 carrot, julienne or shredded

1/2 green onion, sliced

1/4 red bell pepper, julienne

3 olives, pitted and chopped (or capers), optional

Lay the collard green on a flat surface. Spread the cheese or pate on the collard green (if using dressing, then ignore this step). Layer on the sprouts. Then, add the carrot, green onion, and bell pepper. Top with the olives. If you're using dressing, put it on now. Fold or roll up the sandwich and eat it. If you need to save the sandwich and take it with you to go, then use tooth picks to hold it together.

Variations:

- Add a small handful of raisins or currants
- Replace the carrot with shredded apple
- Use a nori sheet instead of the collard green. Once you've assembled your nutritious sandwich, slice it in half or into mini-rolls. Use the left over dressing as a dipping sauce
- Add soaked and slivered sun-dried tomatoes
- Add chopped mushrooms
- Swap out the collard green and use grape leaves for the wrap

BEACH FRONT WRAP

Yield 1 serving

    1 collard green
    2 tablespoons *Crème Fraiche* (see recipe, p.25)
    1 handful alfalfa sprouts
    1/4 mango, peeled, pitted, and julienne
    1/2 banana, peeled, and sliced
    1/2 green onion, sliced
    1 tablespoon dried, unsweetened coconut
    juice of 1 fresh lime

72

Lay the collard green on a flat surface. Spread the *Crème Fraiche* on the collard green. Next, put on the sprouts. Then, layer the mango, banana slices, and green onion. Top with the shredded coconut. Squeeze the fresh lime juice on top of the wrap. Fold or roll up the sandwich and eat it. If you need to save the sandwich and take it with you to go, then omit the banana, add more mango and use tooth picks to hold it together.

Variations:

- Add some freshly chopped pineapple
- Sprinkle a pinch of cinnamon and/or allspice
- Add a pinch of cayenne pepper
- Add young Thai coconut meat, julienne

CREAMY CURRY SAUCE WITH VEGETABLES

Yield approximately 2 cups sauce

This is a scrumptious sauce that is perfect with a plateful of chopped veggies for a wonderful meal.

3/4 cup water

2 avocados, pitted and peeled

1 orange, peeled, seeded

1 clove garlic

juice of 1 lime

1/2 teaspoon Himalayan crystal salt

2 teaspoons curry powder

1/4 teaspoon cinnamon

Blend all of the ingredients until creamy. Serve over your favorite chopped veggies.

TWILIGHT PECAN SHALLOT PATE

See photo at KristensRaw.com/photos.

Yield 2 cups

This is so full of rich flavor and really easy to make. It's one of the best pates when introducing someone new to Raw food... especially meat eaters because it's extremely satisfying and hearty.

2 cups pecans
1 cup spinach
2 tablespoons shallot, chopped
1 tablespoon tamari, wheat-free
2 cloves garlic, pressed
2 tablespoons fresh lemon juice
1 1/2 teaspoons dried marjoram
1/8 teaspoon black pepper

Grind the pecans in a food processor, fitted with the "S" blade, until coarsely ground. Add the remaining ingredients and pulse until well combined (I like it as a crumbly texture). Twilight Pecan Shallot Pate will keep for about four days when stored in an airtight container in the refrigerator or up to six months in the freezer.

Serving suggestions:

- Serve in a romaine lettuce wrap topped with freshly diced tomatoes and sprouts. Yum!
- Stuff this in half of a seeded orange, red, or yellow bell pepper (or tomato) – as shown in the photo. This is one of my favorites ☺
- Serve in cucumber or zucchini boats
- Simply eat by the spoonful. Works for me!
- Use as "meat" stuffing in *No-Meat Rawvioli (see recipe, p. 53)*

GOURMET ITALIAN QUICHE TARTS

See photo at KristensRaw.com/photos.

Yield 8 small tarts

These are truly decadent and gourmet with the play of flavors and textures, yet really simple to make! I promise.

I served these for one of our family holiday dinners last year and every one of the non-Raw vegans at the table were practically licking their plates when they were done. I should have taken pictures of that (ha ha!).

The Crusts

1/2 cup chia meal (approximately 1/3 cup chia seeds)

1/2 cup flax meal (approximately 1/3 cup flax seeds)

2 cups zucchini, peeled and chopped

1/2 cup olive oil

1 3/4 teaspoon Himalayan crystal salt

(continued)

zest from one lemon

1/8 teaspoon cayenne pepper

1 cup walnuts, soaked 6 hours, drained and rinsed

The Filling

1 cup water

1 cup red bell pepper, chopped

1 cup zucchini, peeled and chopped

2 large cloves garlic

2 tablespoons miso (I love the unique varieties offered by South River Miso for extra flavorful results)*

2 tablespoons tamari, wheat-free

1 tablespoon nutritional yeast

3 tablespoons lemon juice

1/4 teaspoon turmeric

1 tablespoon onion powder

2 cups cashews, unsoaked

1 cup basil, packed

10 kalamata olives, chopped

1/2 cup sun-dried tomatoes, soaked 1 hour, drained

2 tablespoons psyllium powder

The Crust Directions

If you haven't already done so, use a dry blender to grind the chia and flax seeds into a meal and set aside in a large bowl.

Blend the zucchini, olive oil, salt, lemon zest and cayenne until smooth. Add the soaked walnuts and blend until creamy.

Pour the blended mixture into the bowl with the chia and flax meal. Stir together. Using two dehydrator trays lined with paraflex non-stick sheets, place 1/3 cup of the batter into 4 mounds (per tray). Using an offset spatula, spread the mounds into flat rounds. Gently lift up the outer edge of each crust so that it forms an edge (which you'll later flute). Dehydrate them at 135 degrees for 45 minutes. Flute the crusts by using the index finger of your left hand and the index finger and thumb on your right hand.

Place them back into the dehydrator and lower the temperature to 105 degrees and dehydrate another 4 - 6 hours. Using a spatula, gently remove them from the paraflex sheet and place them on the normal dehydrator mesh tray and continue dehydrating another 6 - 8 hours, or until dry. These freeze great so you can make them ahead of time. (I freeze them in Food Saver bags by carefully using the Food Saver to remove most, but not all, of the air, so they don't get crushed in the process.)

The Filling Directions

Blend the water, red bell pepper, zucchini, garlic, miso, tamari, nutritional yeast, lemon juice, turmeric, and onion powder until creamy. Add the cashews and blend until smooth. Add the basil, olives and sun-dried tomatoes and pulse to mix. Add the psyllium powder and pulse to blend briefly.

Fill the dehydrated crusts with the mixture and dehydrate for approximately 1 hour at 125 degrees to warm, if desired, or serve as is. Store these in an airtight container for up to four days. (The filling freezes well, too, so you can make this ahead of time and then simply assemble and dehydrate the quiche tarts when you want.)

* Available at SouthRiverMiso.com

Variations:

- If you have leftover filling, this makes an exquisite dip for vegetable crudités. Or, you can spread a thick layer of it on a paraflex non-stick sheet and dehydrate for 3 - 4 hours to make an omelet type breakfast dish.
- As an alternative to make the process a little quicker, you can make 4 larger quiche tarts and cut them in half before serving.

SAVORY PROTEIN STUFFED MUSHROOMS

Yield 16 - 20 stuffed mushrooms

When my friends and family have a party, they *always* ask me to bring this as one my dishes.

The Mushrooms & Marinade

16 - 20 mushrooms

1/4 cup hemp oil

1 tablespoon tamari, wheat-free

1 tablespoon fresh lime juice

The Stuffing

> 3/4 cup hemp seeds
>
> 3/4 cup zucchini, chopped
>
> 1/2 cup carrot, chopped
>
> 1/2 cup parsley or cilantro, packed
>
> 1 large clove garlic, chopped
>
> 1/2 teaspoon cumin
>
> Juice of 1/2 lime
>
> 2 teaspoons tamari, wheat-free

The Marinade Directions

Wipe the mushrooms clean by using a damp paper towel or dish towel. Put the marinade ingredients in a glass baking dish and briefly whisk together. Cut a light "X" in the top surface of each mushroom and place the mushrooms "X" side down in the glass baking dish so the marinade is able to get absorbed into the "X." Let them set in the marinade while you make the stuffing.

The Stuffing Directions

Place all of the ingredients in a food processor, fitted with the "S" blade, and process until semi-smooth. It's nice not to process completely or the colors blend too much. I like to see flecks of color; therefore, I process the ingredients most of the way, while leaving some flecks of color and texture. Use 1 - 2 teaspoons and stuff the mushrooms. These are ready to eat.

To make them extra gourmet and delicious, place them in your dehydrator at 135 degrees for 45 minutes and enjoy slightly warmed (or, at this point you can lower the temperature to 105 degrees and continue dehydrating another 1 - 2 hours, until you're ready to eat).

Store any leftover stuffing in an airtight container in the refrigerator for up to four days. You can store leftover Savory Protein Stuffed Mushrooms in an airtight container in the refrigerator for two days (reheat in your dehydrator if desired).

CHAPTER 3

BREADS, CRACKERS & BARS

STORAGE TIP

In general, Raw vegan breads and crackers will keep for up to one month or longer, if stored in an airtight container in the refrigerator. They'll last up to six months or more if you store them in the freezer in an airtight container.

KITCHEN SINK CRACKERS AND BREAD

The premise here is to know that anything you find Raw and "leftover" in your refrigerator can pretty much be used to make crackers and bread. They can consist of everything but the kitchen sink – ha ha. I love experimenting with my Kitchen Sink recipes. It makes me feel like a chemist. ☺

You need some kind of seed, with the ability to bind well, to begin. Flax and Chia seeds are perfect for this (whole, ground, or a mixture). Next, select a non-binding type of seed such as sunflower seeds, pumpkin seeds, sesame seeds, or a combination of them. Grind them a bit and add to the bowl with the binding seeds.

Next, I look in my refrigerator for veggies and/or fresh fruit. I put them in a blender with about 1/2 cup water to start (adding more if necessary) and blend them up. This could include garlic, herbs, zucchini, tomatoes, celery, beets, olives, ginger, lime and lemon juice, banana, apple, carrots, etc. ...

any, or all, of these things. Just get creative and don't be scared. It's empowering!

Blend them up and transfer them to the seed mixture and mix well by hand. You'll need enough of the dry, ground seeds so that when you add the blended mixture and stir it, a batter type consistency is formed. If you find that the batter is too "wet" then stir in some more ground chia or flax seeds to make it thicker and absorb some of the water.

You can spread them out immediately for dehydrating, or you can let them sit on your countertop for a few hours, where the mixture will soak into the seeds even more and "rise" a little. Then, spread 2 - 2 1/2 cups of the "batter" on paraflex dehydrator sheet(s). *For a cracker-like result, spread the batter thin, about 1/8-inch, maybe a little more. If you want a more bread-like result, make the batter about 1/4 - 1/2-inch thick or more.*

If possible, score the crackers into desired size now, and dehydrate them at 140 degrees for one hour. If you can't score them yet because they're too wet, score them after dehydrating for an hour at 140 degrees. Then, reduce the temperature to 105 and dehydrate another 6 - 8 hours. Flip the crackers over and remove the paraflex sheet. Dehydrate them for another 8 - 24 hours, until the desired dryness is achieved.

BASIC CHIA SEED CRACKERS

Yield depends on the size you cut and amount made

Start with 1 part chia and/or flax seeds combined with 2 parts water in a bowl. To flavor them, stir in 1 tablespoon of dried seasoning, or 3 tablespoons of fresh seasoning, per 1 cup of dry seeds that you use. Add more or less as desired, but remember that flavors are enhanced when dehydrated so you might need less than you think. This is especially noticed when using garlic, salt and spice.

After adding your desired flavors, allow the mixture to sit for an hour to become gelatinous. Then, spread the mixture on dehydrator paraflex sheets. If possible, score the crackers into desired size now, and dehydrate them at 140 degrees for one hour. If you can't score them yet because they're to wet, score them after dehydrating for an hour at 140 degrees. Then, reduce the temperature to 105 degrees for about 8 - 10 hours (depending on thickness).

Flip over to facilitate drying on the other side for another 6 - 10 hours (or more), but this time they can go straight onto the mesh dehydrator sheet. Depending on the ingredients added, it might have a crispy texture or a crispy/chewy texture.

Flavor Possibilities

Plain

Garlic, Himalayan crystal salt

Rosemary, thyme, basil

Cinnamon, vanilla, agave (or Rapadura®)

Fresh lime juice, rosemary, mint

Garlic, salt, basil

Pizza flavors

Spicy red pepper

Curry, cardamom, turmeric, ginger

KRISTEN SUZANNE'S ADDICTIVE SAVORY MUSTARD BREAD

Yield 3 dehydrator trays of bread

It's nearly impossible to only eat one piece of this. In fact, I have clients emailing me all the time asking me to make it.

3 1/2 pounds of onions, peeled and chopped
3 medium tomatoes, chopped
1 cup flax meal
1/2 cup pumpkin seeds, ground
1/2 cup sunflower seeds, ground
1/3 cup nutritional yeast
1/4 cup *Raw Mustard* (see p. 26)*
1/2 cup raw agave nectar
1/2 cup tamari wheat-free

Process the onions and tomatoes in a food processor, fitted with the "S" blade, into small pieces, but don't let it get to a mush. Set aside in a large bowl and stir in the flax meal and ground pumpkin and sunflower seeds.

Add the remaining ingredients and mix well by hand. Use 2 - 3 cups of batter and spread onto each paraflex dehydrator sheet. Dehydrate for one hour at 140 degrees. Lower the temperature for the remainder of the dehydrating time to 105 degrees. Dehydrate for another 6 - 8 hours. Flip the bread over, remove the paraflex sheet and dehydrate another 6 - 10 hours until the desired dryness is achieved. Cut into whichever size you like using a knife or pizza cutter.

* You can use regular, store-bought mustard (not Raw) if you don't have *Raw Mustard* prepared.

Serving suggestions:

- Enjoy this amazing bread with all kinds of cheeze spreads, hummus, or eat it plain (it's so full of flavor)

- It also makes a terrific pizza crust!

BANANA HEMP PROTEIN BARS

Yield 1 - 2 dehydrator trays full (depending on thickness desired)

My husband was worried about getting enough protein and calories in this diet, even though the World Health Organization agrees we need a mere 10% of our calories from protein. I made these for him anyway.

2 cups water

2 cups hemp protein powder

2 bananas, peeled and chopped

1 apple, cored and chopped

1 tablespoon raw agave nectar

1 teaspoon vanilla extract

3/4 teaspoon cinnamon

1/2 teaspoon Himalayan crystal salt

1 cup flax meal

1 banana, peeled, sliced and set aside

Blend all the ingredients together in a blender, except for the flax meal and the one sliced banana you set aside. Pour the mixture into a large bowl and stir in the flax meal. Fold in the sliced banana.

Spread the mixture onto a paraflex dehydrator sheet. If you're looking for a thicker, chewier bar, make it 3/4-inch to 1-inch thick. Score the bars into the desired shape. Dehydrate at 140 degrees for 1 - 2 hours. Decrease the temperature to 105 degrees and continue dehydrating another 6 - 10 hours. Flip bars onto the *mesh* dehydrator sheet and continue dehydrating another 6 - 8 hours or longer until you get the desired dryness in your bars.

Serving suggestion:

- For a satisfying meal, use 2 slices of this as sandwich bread and spread hemp butter on one slice and *Sweet Berry Jam* (see recipe, p. 41) on the other slice. Serve an apple on the side and call it a great protein-rich meal!

VANILLA HEMP PROTEIN BARS

Yield 1 - 2 dehydrator trays full (depending on thickness desired)

These are a fantastic variation of my hemp bars, but with a little vanilla flavor!

2 cups water

2 cups hemp powder

2 apples, cored and chopped

2 tablespoons raw agave nectar

1 teaspoon vanilla extract

1 teaspoon cinnamon

1 vanilla bean, minced

pinch Himalayan crystal salt

1 cup flax meal

Blend all of the ingredients together, except the flax meal, in a blender. Pour the mixture into a large bowl and stir in the flax meal.

Spread the mixture onto a paraflex dehydrator sheet. If you're looking for a thicker, chewier bar, make it 3/4 - 1-inch thick. Score into the desired shape. Dehydrate at 140 degrees for 1 - 2 hours. Decrease the temperature to 105 degrees and continue dehydrating another 6 - 10 hours. Flip the bars onto the mesh dehydrator sheet and continue dehydrating another 6 - 8 hours or longer until you get the desired dryness in your bars.

Serving suggestion:

- These are delicious slathered with *Sweet Berry Jam* (see recipe, p. 41) and then topped with sliced banana. Delectable!

CHOCOLATE SNACK BREAD

Yield approximately 2 dehydrator trays

This is a great alternative to ordinary flax bread. The chocolate flavor is subtle so you can eat it with pretty much anything.

    1 3/4 cups flax seeds
    3/4 cup raw chocolate powder
    1 cup water
    1 apple, cored and chopped
    1 banana, peeled and chopped
    1/4 cup raw agave nectar
    1 teaspoon Himalayan crystal salt
    1/4 teaspoon cinnamon
    1/2 teaspoon vanilla

Grind the flax seeds to a meal and set aside in a large bowl. Stir in the raw chocolate powder. Blend the water, apple, banana, agave, salt, cinnamon, and vanilla. Add the blended mixture to the chocolate and flax mixture. Stir by hand. If you're mixture is too "wet" just add a little more ground flax seed.

Spread the mixture onto a dehydrator paraflex sheet. If you want crackers, spread the batter thinner (approximately 1/8 to 1/4-inch thick). For a more "bread-like" result, spread a thicker batter (approximately 1/4 to 1/2-inch thick, or more). If possible, score the mixture to the desired size and shape you want. If it's too wet to score, then score after the first 1 - 2 hours of dehydrating. Dehydrate for 1 hour at 140 degrees. Lower the temperature and dehydrate another 6 - 8 hours at 105 degrees. Flip the bread over onto the mesh sheets and continue dehydrating another 6 - 12 hours, or until you reach your desired dryness.

Serving suggestion:

- I love eating these with any kind of raw nut/seed butter (hazelnut, hemp, pecan, macadamia, etc) and my *Sweet Berry Jam* (see recipe, p. 41). Kids love these!

GARLIC BASIL FLAX CRACKERS

Yield approximately 12 crackers

    1 cup flax meal
    1/4 cup olive oil
    1/4 cup water, more if needed

(continued)

1/4 cup basil leaves

2 - 3 cloves garlic

1 tablespoon fresh lemon juice

1 - 2 tablespoons raw agave nectar, optional

1/2 teaspoon Himalayan crystal salt

1/2 teaspoon onion powder

pinch black pepper

Place the flax meal into a large bowl and set aside. Blend the remaining ingredients together and add it to the bowl with the flax meal. Mix well by hand (adding a little more water if needed). Spread onto a paraflex dehydrator sheet about 1/8 to 1/4-inch thick. Dehydrate for 1 hour at 140 degrees. Lower the temperature for the remainder of the dehydrating time to 105 degrees. Dehydrate for another 6 - 8 hours. Flip them over, remove the paraflex sheet and dehydrate another 6 - 12 hours (or more) until desired dryness is achieved. Cut into desired shape and size.

Serving suggestion:

- I love using these for pizza crusts when I'm not munching on them as crackers

SWEET-N-SAVORY BREAD

Yield approximately 3 dehydrator trays of bread

This is another one of my favorite Raw recipes. It's delicious, easy to make, and complements almost any recipe to make a wonderful meal.

4 pounds sweet yellow onions, peeled and chopped

2 bananas, peeled and chopped

1 cup flax meal

1 cup pumpkin seeds, ground

1/3 cup tamari, wheat-free

1/3 cup extra virgin olive oil

2 tablespoons fresh lemon juice

Process the onions and bananas in a food processor, fitted with the "S" blade, into small pieces, but don't let it get to a mush. Set aside in a large bowl and stir in the flax meal and ground pumpkin seeds. Add the remaining ingredients and mix well by hand. Use 2 - 3 cups of the batter and spread about 1/4-inch thick onto paraflex dehydrator sheets.

Dehydrate for one hour at 140 degrees. Lower the temperature for the remainder of the dehydrating time to 105 degrees. Dehydrate for another 6 - 8 hours. Flip the bread over onto the mesh sheets, remove the paraflex sheet and dehydrate another 6 - 10 hours or until the desired dryness is achieved. Cut into desired shape and size.

COCONUT TORTILLA WRAPS

Yield approximately 4 medium tortilla wraps

2 cups young Thai coconut meat (about 3 - 4 coconuts)

1 1/2 cups young Thai coconut water, more if necessary

1/2 cup hemp powder

(continued)

1/2 teaspoon poultry seasoning or any other seasoning of your choice

dash Himalayan crystal salt

1/2 cup flax meal

Blend all of the ingredients, except for the flax meal, until smooth. Add the flax meal and blend briefly to incorporate.

Spread the mixture on a dehydrator paraflex sheet, in the desired size of tortilla rounds. Dehydrate at 140 degrees for about 30 minutes. Lower the temperature to 105 degrees and dehydrate another few hours. Gently lift them up to see if they're ready to flip. If they're ready, then flip them onto the mesh dehydrator sheets so the other side dries. Dehydrate another few hours, until they're pliable, but not crispy dry or they won't wrap around your food. If you dehydrate them too far, get a spray bottle and mist them lightly with water until they become pliable for you.

Serving suggestion:

- Use these for wrap sandwiches stuffed with any of the following - guacamole, minced vegetables, salsa, sea vegetables, shredded fruit, etc.

Breinigsville, PA USA
08 January 2010
230416BV00004B/49/P